In Your
Dreams

In Your Dreams

By Julia Marsden

SCHOLASTIC INC.
New York Toronto London Auckland Sydney
Mexico City New Delhi Hong Kong

ISBN 0-439-16117-7
Copyright © 2000 by Scholastic Inc.

Published by Scholastic Inc.,
555 Broadway, New York, NY 10012.

SCHOLASTIC and associated logos are trademarks
and/or registered trademarks of Scholastic Inc.

12 11 10 9 8 7 6 5 4 3 2 1   0 1 2 3 4 5/0

Printed in the U.S.A.   01
First Scholastic printing, April 2000

Table of Contents

In Your Dreams

Introduction

Picture this: You've lost consciousness and relinquished all control over your thoughts. Plus, your body has become as rigid as a statue. Sound like some strange alien abduction or an episode of *The X-Files*? Hardly. It happens to you every night when you fall asleep! And even though this description of how things go when you're in a dream state may sound like some weird alien abduction episode, you'll see why it's really apt when you read this book.

A few of the things you're about to find out include what happens to your brain when you're sleeping, what certain symbols in your dreams mean, and how to decipher and decode your dreams using the A to Z Dream Dictionary (see Chapter Four).

Ready for an amazing look at the overnight sensation known as dreaming? Then read on to discover all about sleep and dreams!

Dream On!

Chapter One
The Dreamers Hall of Fame

*L*ots of famous writers, musicians, poets, and artists have experienced creative dreams that helped them start or complete projects they were working on. The author and poet Robert Louis Stevenson totally tapped into his dreams to help him create his poems and stories. He experienced tons of nightmares as a little boy, and as he got older he had lots of dreams about adventures and journeys. In fact, it got to the point where he would dream entire stories each night, and sometimes a story that started one night would continue where it left off the next night!

When these ongoing dream stories kept happening, Stevenson was so freaked out he started to think he was leading a double life. And that feeling of living a double life became the inspiration for his famous novel *The Strange Case of Dr. Jekyll and Mr. Hyde*! And famous author Mary Shelley, who was into creating spooky stories way before Stephen King came on the scene, credited her scary dreams with being the inspiration behind her classic novel *Frankenstein*, which has given readers all over the world goose bumps.

What's Your Problem?

Another type of dream that many famous people have experienced is the problem-solving dream. These dreams offer the dreamer a solution or clue to a problem or puzzle he or she is trying to figure out. For example, Albert Einstein was struggling to solve a particular physics problem. He had spent tons of time trying to work out a solution to an equation. Then one night he went to sleep and had a dream that he was on a sled sailing down a snow-covered slope. He was traveling so fast that as he looked up at the stars they looked like a big blur in the sky. When Einstein woke up, he had his answer. He realized the dream was telling him how the speed of light can distort matter, and this led to his amazing work on the theory of relativity!

Here's another weird dream discovery from history. An American inventor named Elias Howe wanted to design a sewing machine but he couldn't quite figure out how to go about creating it. Then while he was sleeping he had a dream about being chased by a bunch of guys carrying spears! He raced away from the guys, who were raising their spears and jabbing them up and down. He noticed that each spear had a little hole at the top, and just as he was about to be stabbed in his dream he woke up with his invention all figured out. He realized the sewing machine had to have a needle with a hole in it for thread to pass through and that the needle should move up and down through the fabric.

And here's another: A chemist named August Kekule was trying to figure out how the molecules in a particular chemical fit together. Then one night he had a dream about a snake that was trying to bite its own tail. He woke up with his answer. He realized that the chemical's molecular structure formed a ring!

What's the secret to dream problem-solving? It could be concentrating very hard on something you're hoping to solve. Say you've got a stressful situation you're trying to sort out that concerns a friend who's been bugging you. You really want to come up with a solution that will help smooth things out between the two of you. Before you go to bed, you tell yourself you're going to hand over your friendship troubles to your subconscious mind.

After you nod off, your subconscious kicks into high gear and gives your conscious mind a break. And your subconscious doesn't just take into account stuff that's going on in your everyday life. It also grabs on to stuff from your past and tries to relate it to things that are happening in your life now.

By allowing your subconscious to pick up some of the slack, you may wake up with the perfect solution for ironing things out with your pal. You've got to be patient to make this work. You've got to believe that there's a part of your brain that you can't completely control but that is hard at work trying to help you out. When your conscious thoughts and your subconscious team up together, you're way more likely to work through troubles and come up with some awesome solutions.

Eerie Predictions

Another bizarre type of dream is the clairvoyant dream. These dreams clue in the dreamer to something worrisome that will happen in the future. Dream specialists feel that these dreams may be the result of the dreamer's bottled up worries, fears, and anxieties.

Abraham Lincoln experienced one of the most famous predictive dreams in American history. He told a bunch of his friends about a dream in which he was walking through the White House and hearing people crying. But he couldn't see anybody. When he reached the East Room of the White House, he saw a coffin. There were soldiers standing nearby and he approached them and asked, "Who is dead in the White House?" They answered, "The President. He was assassinated." A few days after he told his friends about his dream, Lincoln was killed by John Wilkes Booth!

Another predictive dream that made some major waves occurred in April of 1912. A Norwegian fisherman claimed a voice in his dream told him that a ship would sink after running into an iceberg. He woke from his dream in a panic, fell back to sleep, and then dreamed that icy waves were crashing around his body. Two days later, the *Titanic* sank!

And now for an important message: Don't panic. Typically when people dream about death or dying, it doesn't mean someone is literally going to die. In the world of dreams, death is often just a symbol for change or an end to a particular situation. It can also mean that your enthusiasm for something or someone has "died" or that you're ready to move on in some way.

Direct Your Dreams: The Lowdown on Lucid Dreams

Some of the weirdest dreams you can experience are the ones in which you are aware as you are dreaming that you are dreaming. These are called lucid dreams. Most lucid dreams occur in the morning.

Another bizarre type of experience that's believed to be linked to lucid dreaming is the out-of-body experience (OBE). An OBE usually lasts a very short time when a person's consciousness or thoughts seem to leave her physical body so that she seems to be outside herself looking at herself. Patients in hospitals who have been under anesthesia often report OBEs. To picture what this might be like, think of yourself watching an *ER* episode. Dr. Green is operating on a patient and suddenly on your TV screen you see a shadowy outline of the patient's body hovering over the operating table. Then in a quick flash the patient glides back into her body, and when she wakes up from surgery reports that she had a bird's-eye view of the whole surgical procedure. Wow!

Dreams and Time Travel

Whether you remember your dreams or not, you dream every night. Throughout history, people have always been very curious about the dream scene, and as a result, some very weird beliefs about dreams have cropped up. Ages ago, people thought dreams were the work of the gods or of the devil! Some thought dreams could predict the future. Way before this dream book was written — we're talking 1350 B.C. — the oldest known dream book was written by the Egyptians. And some of the ideas in that book are still being used by researchers who are involved in figuring out dreams today!

Going Greek

Many ancient Greeks believed dreams were divine messages. Aristotle, a Greek philosopher, had a theory that dreams weren't messages from the gods but were a kind of instant replay of a person's day. He was also totally into the idea that dreams contain lots of symbols (images that stand for something else). For example, that dream you had about a cake with candles flying overhead could stand for the fact that your birthday is fast approaching.

The Dream Team: Freud and Jung

Talk about a couple of completely dreamy dudes! Back in the late nineteenth and early twentieth centuries, there were two guys who really got into studying dreams. One was the psychiatrist Sigmund Freud. He started studying dreams when he was working with his patients. They would often tell him about their dreams, and he began to see that their dreams offered lots of valuable insight into their problems.

Freud developed a way for his patients to use their dreams to help them solve their problems as part of a method called psychoanalysis, which involves studying a person's mind and personality. He believed that dreams were kind of like safety valves that allow people to address feelings and ideas they are having that they might not feel comfortable expressing during their waking hours.

Freud also believed that dreams are a way for people to process information about their secret wishes and desires. Lots of people disagree with the theories Freud had about dreams, but lots of stuff he discovered has helped to form the framework for dream analysis today.

The other guy who had a lot to say about dreams and their meanings was Carl Jung. Jung was actually one of Freud's friends, but he didn't agree with him on everything. He didn't believe that dreams are necessarily wishes the dreamer wants to come true. And Jung believed that it was totally possible for people to have dreams about things they don't know about or have never been exposed to. He felt that people can inherit dream symbols from generations before them. Jung called this the "collective unconscious." He felt this was the reason people all over the world have very similar symbols appear in their dreams even though their lives and experiences are quite different. He also was a big believer in how images from legends and fairy tales appear as dream symbols for just about everybody. Some dream symbols that almost everybody has are kings and queens, paths, bridges, houses, and shadows. In fact, so many people experience dreams with these particular symbols that they've been dubbed "universal symbols."

Chapter Two
Dream Details by the Dozen

What's Your Position?

Odds are you sleep in one particular position once you're snoozing. There are various ways to sleep, but sleep experts have narrowed them down to several basic postures. Some sleep experts believe that the position you sleep in says certain things about your personality. Check out the following descriptions and see which one sounds most like you.

Your Position: **The Flip Sider** (prone)
You sleep on your stomach, as if to announce that you have taken over the entire territory of your bed.

Your Personality: You tend to be a private person. Sleeping on your stomach is a way for you to feel safe and in control. You don't feel comfortable revealing too much of yourself to others.

Your Position: **The Mummy**

You sleep wrapped up in your covers, as if to escape from the world.

Your Personality: You like to feel secure and tend to surround yourself with people who support you and stand by you. You are sometimes slow to let down your guard around new people.

Your Position: **The Baby** (semi-fetal)

You sleep tucked in a ball in much the same way a baby is positioned inside a mother's womb.

Your Personality: You need lots of attention and love. When you're not curled up and asleep, you like clutching a pillow or favorite stuffed animal that's super-sentimental to you. Like Linus from *Peanuts*, you like having a "security blanket." You give all you've got to your family and friends and they seem to know how emotional you can be. You're very in touch with your feelings and sensitive toward others.

Your Position: **The Boxer**

You sleep on your back with your hands clutching the covers as if you're "putting up your dukes."

Your Personality: You're pretty outgoing but there's a part of you that likes to keep things to yourself. You're open to meeting new people and trying new things but like to gravitate back to things that are familiar.

Your Position: **The Royal**
You sleep on your back, arms stretched out on either side of your body.
Your Personality: Sleeping on your back shows that you're open to what life brings your way. You're seen as an outgoing and fun friend. You have no problem being in the limelight. You tend to be pretty self-confident.

Your Position: **The Side Sleeper**
First off, you're not alone. About 60 percent of all people sleep on their sides.
Your Personality: You're a laid-back person who is seen as being flexible and into compromise. Your "let's work it out" attitude makes you a favorite among your friends.

Girls and Guys: What's the Difference?

Girls tend to dream more about females. Women and girls appear more in girls' dreams than in guys' dreams.

Guys tend to dream more about males. Men and guys appear more in guys' dreams than in girls' dreams.

Relationships, houses, clothing, and jewelry appear more in girls' dreams than they do in guys' dreams.

Cars, tools, sports, and action adventures appear more in guys' dreams than they do in girls' dreams.

Girls are more apt to recognize and be able to name the people who appear in their dreams.

Guys aren't as able to recognize the people who appear in their dreams.

Girls tend to enjoy discussing their dreams with others and find it easy to describe what they dream about.

Guys tend to get embarrassed about discussing their dreams.

Act Your Age!

Just as there are some differences between how girls and guys dream, there are also some differences between how children and adults dream. Little kids tend to dream about animals more than adults do. They also see way more monsters and wild creatures. Remember Maurice Sendak's classic children's book *Where the Wild Things Are*? Talk about depicting a kid's complete dreamworld! Pretty scary stuff when you're a five-year-old! Kids also experience a ton more nightmares than adults do. Go ahead. You can 'fess up to those times when you ran into your mom and dad's bedroom, wiggled your way between them, and said, "I had a bad dream."

Some little kids have so many bad dreams, psychologists even refer to these nightmares as night terrors! Yikes! It's a time when toddlers need lots of attention and reassurance. You know the drill. We're talking about those times when you were little and you insisted that a grown-up conduct an under-the-bed and in-the-closet check to confirm that monsters weren't hiding anywhere.

Studies have shown that kids also dream about certain things more than adults do. Some of the top things kids dream about include being threatened by animals or insects, being chased by monsters, flying, falling, being trapped, being tested, or appearing naked in public.

Do You Walk the Walk and Talk the Talk?

Turns out sleepwalking (and talking!) is more common in young people, too. How does that work? Well, if you've ever done it, you're not alone. There are thousands of somnambulists in America (sleepwalkers, that is)! You're not dreaming when you sleepwalk because you can't move when you're dreaming.

You've heard about not being able to walk and chew gum at the same time? Well, you simply can't walk and dream at the same time. Studies show that sleepwalking is an inherited trait, so if an adult in your family has ever sleepwalked, odds are greater that you might, too.

And what's up with people who talk in their sleep? It can be pretty freaky to carry on a conversation with someone you know is asleep. People tend to talk in their sleep when something is troubling them or, conversely, when they are very happy about something.

Here's Some More Weird Dream Data

By the time a baby is twelve months old, he or she will dream up to five hours each night.

Grown-ups dream about two hours each night.

Dreams can last from a few minutes to up to an hour!

If you live to be eighty years old, you will have spent about ten cumulative years of your life dreaming!

Are You a Daydream Believer?

So, what's the deal with daydreams? Do they really count as dreams? When you're daydreaming, you're still conscious so you get to create the script of your dream. (At night, it's as if you're reading a script that's being written by your subconscious. You're watching a movie that's already been finished rather than directing one that's in the process of being made.)

The cool thing about daydreams is that they're structured like stories in the same way that your night dreams are. Try to catch yourself when you're daydreaming. Some studies show that we daydream during 50 to 70 percent of our waking hours.

See if there's a theme to your daydream. Is the story that's playing in your head actually something that's bugging you or something that you're worried about or want?

Study the story. The more you look at the links in your daydreams, the more likely you are to make connections between your daydreams and any issues you're trying to sort out.

What a Nightmare!

Not all dreams are from the dream-come-true department. And if you've ever had one of those

20

dreams that was so supremely scary you woke yourself up before it could go on a second longer, you're not alone. Children are especially prone to scary dreams because they're so young they have a tough time distinguishing between what goes on during the day and what goes on at night when they're sleeping. Teens can experience lots of nightmares, too, because of all the emotional and physical changes that occur during adolescence. But not to worry, adults aren't left out of being scared out of their wits, either. According to research that was done at a sleep research center in Boston, about 50 percent of the adult population experiences one or two nightmares a year, and about 10 percent of adults experience a nightmare once a month.

If you want to bail on the bogeyman or any bad-dream character for that matter, just start walking. Researchers found that a group of females who walked the equivalent of six blocks or more a day reduced their chances of having nightmares by about 75 percent. Physical activity can decrease your stress and anxiety levels, and it's high stress that can be linked to lots of nightmares and disturbed sleep.

What's the deal with nightmares, anyway? Why would we subconsciously want to scare ourselves silly and freak ourselves out so badly that we wake up, hearts racing, arms braced against the bedsheets? Well, apparently nightmares serve a good purpose. They help us to work out frustrations and alert us to things that are subconsciously bothering us when we're awake. They actually have the power to heal!

Nightmares can help you play through certain scenarios and rid yourself of fears or anxious feelings you may be having about something that's going on in your life. Say a teacher at school calls on you and makes you feel really lame for not knowing the answer. That night, you have a nightmare in which you spot your teacher in the hallway as you're standing at your locker. You stick your tongue out at her and she, completely surprised by your behavior, looks stunned. Does this mean you are a completely cruel person? Not at all! It's just your mind allowing you to sort through something that bugged you during the day. It's kind of like your brain's way of saying, "Get over it!" And a nightmare can come with a bonus, too: Once your brain has had a chance to process what happened to you at school, you're much more likely to hit the books and be more on the ball the next time the teacher calls on you. While dreams can be so subtle you have to strain to see the message — nightmares get in your face!

If you're having a lot of nightmares and they're really starting to affect how you feel about going to bed each night, there are ways you can be more in control. Rather than letting the nightmares be in charge, go to bed having decided that you will be the director of your subconscious horror flick.

Here's how: Use your brain to redirect the action in the nightmare. If you're dreaming about being chased by a crazed creature, tell yourself before you fall asleep that if the creature shows up in your sleep, you'll turn around and shout at it. Or tell your brain to recast the creature as a character you like such as your pet or your best friend. The whole tone of the "dream-movie" will change thanks to your expert direction.

And what if you still have a super-scary dream despite your directorial debut in dreamland? If you've been scared awake by a nightmare, replay the bad dream in your mind. Spend enough time thinking about all the grim and ugly details so they become insignificant and not intimidating. When you get to the absolutely freaky part that scared you out of your sleep, rewrite what will happen next. A new ending puts you in charge of how things turn out and will allow you to fall back to sleep more easily.

Chapter Three

The Creatures and Colors in Your Dreams

By now you've read the goods on people and dreams. But what's up with your dog when he's on the floor and his hind legs start twitching in his sleep? And what about your cat, who's clicking her teeth as if she's after a bird? Are your pets dreaming, too?

Sleep researchers and dream experts are pretty certain that most mammals dream. Look closely and you may be able to see your pet's eyes moving under the eyelids.

You can't exactly ask your pets to tell you all about the dreams they've had but there's definitely some evidence that animals do dream. Human brains and animal brains aren't the same but they do have some similarities. Dream researchers say that animals go through stages of sleep, just like humans. But when it comes to all creatures great and small, there are some dream differences. Nocturnal animals sleep and dream during the day. And here's a weird bit of barnyard trivia — horses and cows sleep standing up but they only dream if they're lying down! Weird or what?

Another weird mammal fact — dolphins don't dream. And guess what else? Bottle-nosed dolphins sleep with only half their brains at a time. A Russian scientist discovered that when a dolphin sleeps, each side of its brain takes turns. One half of its brain stays awake while the other half sleeps!

Animals in Your Dreams

So you've shown up to watch your animals dream, but what about the animals that show up in your dreams? Dream experts look to animals as important dream symbols. It turns out most people dream about domestic animals more than wild ones. When you dream about a household pet, you may actually be dreaming about yourself in some way. Your cat or dog could symbolize you! Freud believed that dreams about wild animals symbolized our own desires and wishes and sometimes wild thoughts that live in our subconscious.

Want to know which animals make the top of the animals-in-dreams Hit Parade? Dogs, cats, and horses are at the top of the chart. And females tend to dream about horses more than males.

To figure out dreams about animals, keep in mind that the animals you dream about convey information about what that particular animal means to you. If you were once chased by a dog in your neighborhood, dreaming about a dog is going to mean something very different to you than it does to your friend who's helped train guide dogs for the blind as part of a 4-H project. With that in mind, here are some of the basic reads on animals in your dreams:

Dogs are believed to symbolize faithfulness.

Cats are believed to symbolize wisdom.

Rats are believed to symbolize deception.

Mules are believed to symbolize stubbornness.

Elephants are believed to symbolize memories and the past.

Lions are believed to symbolize bravery and courage.

Bears are believed to symbolize strength, especially in the face of danger.

Buffalo are believed to symbolize power.

Ants are believed to symbolize hard work and perseverance.

Bulls are believed to symbolize forcefulness and anger.

Camels are believed to symbolize obedience and cautiousness.

Mice are believed to symbolize shyness or timidity.

Tigers are believed to symbolize assertiveness.

Pigs are believed to symbolize greed.

A Little Bit About the Birds and the Bees (and the Bugs)

All creatures, great and small, that appear in your dreams are worthy of note. For example, birds in dreams often symbolize freedom, your aspirations, and your spirituality. Dreams of winged creatures such as unicorns or dragons can symbolize a need for you to be released from a situation that's holding you back or a desire to break away from feelings of being restricted. Here are some more insights into the winged creatures of your dreams:

Bats can symbolize an inability to see a situation clearly or an instinctive ability to create your own sense of direction.

Caged birds can symbolize feeling confined.

Chickens can symbolize anxiety.

Roosters can symbolize vigilance or a need to communicate a message.

Doves can symbolize peace and love.

Parrots can symbolize imitation, mimicking, and mocking.

Eagles can symbolize victory.

Hawks can symbolize observation abilities or a desire to see a situation from all angles.

Ostriches can symbolize hiding from a problem in your life.

Owls can symbolize wisdom.

Peacocks can symbolize self-confidence and pride.

Swans can symbolize grace but also a sense of not being recognized for your efforts.

Being stung by a bee or other insect can symbolize being hurt by a situation or someone in your life.

Caterpillars can symbolize a desire to change your present situation.

Butterflies can symbolize a desire to change or improve your image or appearance.

Flies can symbolize irritation or annoyance you may be feeling due to particular people in your life who are pestering you and "getting in your face."

Gnats can symbolize irritations in your life.

Moths can symbolize suspicion or as yet unseen damage that may be occurring.

Spiderwebs can symbolize certain complexities in your life.

Color-coded Dreams

Take a quick poll of the people in your life and see who dreams in color. Most people do. When you start studying your own dreams, the colors that appear can have total significance. Dream experts are convinced that when a certain color appears in a dream in a really intense, take-notice way, it's worth paying attention.

If you think color doesn't help to complete the picture, let's talk about a girl from Kansas we all know. She goes to sleep. She starts dreaming, and suddenly she's got on some new shoes, she's walking down a trail, and she's headed for a new place. Now switch from that boring black-and-white account to the totally Technicolor tale and you may remember the girl's name is Dorothy, she's wearing **RUBY** slippers, walking down a **YELLOW** brick road on her way to the **EMERALD** City. Now *that* covers a much bigger spectrum! If you want to figure out a rainbow of revelations in your dreams, the following are some pointers to help you break through the color codes:

Blue has different meanings depending on the shade of blue you see in your dream, but all are believed to be linked to your moods. Sky blue is believed to be associated with ambition, as in "the sky's the limit." Medium blue is linked with peacefulness and a sense of feeling calm and collected. Dark blue can signify that something is weighing heavily on your mind.

Green is believed to be associated with nature and can signify that you are tuned in to your environment. Dreaming about a green lawn or lots of green plants and trees can be viewed as a sign that things that are bothering you are going to work out. If green appears in a way that seems to be linked with people, it can symbolize jealousy in some form, as in "green with envy."

Orange is believed to be associated with optimism. Orange can be an indication that you should pursue your goals or follow your instincts regarding something that's going on in your life.

Purple is believed to be associated with authority and law. It may appear to help give you guidance about a decision you need to make or offer insight about whether something that's going on in your life is fair.

Red is believed to be associated with love . . . or anger. It's a hot and intense color and the way it appears in your dream determines the meaning.

Yellow is believed to be associated with happiness. It is viewed as a hopeful and optimistic sign when it appears in a dream.

White is believed to be associated with new beginnings. It's considered a hopeful and positive sign when it appears in dreams.

Black is believed to be associated with going through a difficult time. If you're seeing a lot of black in your dreams, it could be you are feeling sad about something.

Before you go to bed each night, think about other colors you would like to see appear in your dreams.

What's Your Number?

As with colors, when specific numbers seem to stand out in your dreams, you might want to take note of what they could mean or symbolize. Say you have a dream in which seven chickens come up to the front door of your house. Sure, you should take note of the fact that chickens are at the door, but also be aware of the fact that *seven* chickens have showed up. And then ask yourself, "Why seven?"

The following are what the numbers 1 through 10 can symbolize:

1   **The number 1** is associated with leadership and winning. It also stands for the self. If a 1 appears a lot in your dream, it could be alluding to you specifically or it may be conveying that you are in the lead in some way. The number 1 is also linked with communication. It could be a clue that you're not getting your point across to someone in your life.

2   **The number 2** is associated with relationships and balance. If you have a dream in which the number 2 plays a prominent role, it could be an indicator that an important relationship in your life is in need of more attention.

3 **The number 3** is associated with creativity. If you dream about the number 3 it could be a clue that you are currently feeling very creative or that you need to tap into your creative talents. The number 3 can also be a sign of indecision. There may be something you've been waffling about, and it may be a sign that it's time to make up your mind — one way or the other.

4 **The number 4** is associated with dependability. In a dream it could be a reminder to yourself to remain dedicated to something you're working on and to remain grounded and rooted. It can also indicate determination.

5 **The number 5** is associated with learning but also with fun. It is believed to be an optimistic number.

6 **The number 6** is associated with family. It also can represent honesty and trustworthiness. It is often a number linked with weddings and lifelong relationships.

7   **The number 7** is associated with inspiration and invention. However, it's also linked with blurting out your opinions in a way that can be hurtful to others.

8   **The number 8** is associated with wealth. Accruing wealth often has a lot to do with the other things associated with 8 . . . hard work, patience, and ambition!

9   **The number 9** is associated with knowledge, independence, and optimism. It can also indicate things that are unpredictable.

10   **The number 10** is associated with perfection.

Dreamscapes: Oh, the Places You'll Go!

Dreams can really take you places. And often the location where you land in a dream can have special meaning, too. Check out what some of the most common dream landscapes may mean:

A forest can represent your unconscious — thoughts and feelings you're not expressing.

A river can represent peace and serenity.

A mountain can represent your aspirations.

A crossroad can represent a decision you need to make.

A storm can represent anger in your life.

A cliff can represent a problem you are hoping to solve.

A desert can represent isolation or feeling deserted. It can also be a sign of something in your life that needs attention or nurturing.

Dreaming
A to Z

Chapter Four
Your Dream Dictionary

This section is all about the language of dreams. Check it out whenever you're wondering what a subject or a certain something in one of your dreams might mean. *A majorly important point:* Every person's dreams are unique, so any dream interpretation you ever read is only one way of looking at things. Nothing's set in stone. The way to use these pages is to read up on some of the more standard dream symbols and then draw your own conclusions. That's the way to develop a better understanding of yourself and your dreams. So, dream on!

A

Accident: You may be experiencing some anxiety about a relationship in your life.

Adventure: You may be about to hear some positive news.

Air: You may be wanting to clear the air

about something or develop a clearer understanding of a situation in your life.

Airplane: You may be ready to try a new experience or see things from a new vantage point.

Alley: You may be concerned about what seems to be an inescapable problem, or you may be about to discover a way out of a situation that's been occupying your thoughts.

Angel: You may be about to experience peace and prosperity or you may be concerned about some of your conduct and behavior.

Applause: You may be seeking recognition for as yet unnoticed accomplishments.

Armor: You may be feeling kind of defensive about something. Or it could be you're not feeling completely confident and feel that you need to "keep your guard up."

Astronaut: You may be interested in testing your boundaries, or perhaps you're in search of something that seems impossible for others to comprehend.

Athletics: You may be feeling confident and sure of yourself. You may also feel there is challenge or competition in your life.

Audition: You may feel you are facing a test of some kind. How the audition goes in your dream may signify how you should deal with a situation in real life.

B

Baby: You may be feeling secure and happy.

Baby-sitter: You may be feeling insecure.

Baggage: You may feel that you have a lot of responsibilities and burdens.

Banquet: You may be focusing on the details instead of on the bigger events in your life.

Bath: You may be feeling a bit guilty about something.

Beach: You may be focusing on a wish you want to come true.

Book: You may be thinking about success and riches. It could also be that you're hoping to reach a better understanding of something.

Bride: You may be thinking about events in your future.

Butterfly: You may be thinking about escaping your troubles or about the spirit or soul of a loved one.

C

Calculator: You may be trying to "calculate" or evaluate some aspect of your life.

Candle: You may be seeking comfort, particularly spiritual comfort.

Castle: You may be feeling safe from your rivals.

Cathedral: You may be concerned about your spiritual life and in search of answers or spiritual guidance.

Cemetery: You may be thinking about loved ones who have passed away or perhaps you're yearning for days in your past.

Circle: You may be thinking about things that, for now, are simply unknowable. Circles tend to symbolize infinity.

Classroom: You may be focused on learning or competition.

Cliff: You may be apprehensive about a current situation or a decision you're faced with.

Clock: You may feel that you are running out of time.

Clown: You may be fearful about making a fool of yourself.

Coat: You may wish to conceal something or keep a secret.

Crystal ball: You may be wishing for something special in your future.

D

Dancer: You may be feeling happy and triumphant.

Desert island: You may feel that you are lacking direction about something in your life.

Door: An open door may indicate an opportunity that is being presented to you; a closed door may indicate that you are feeling isolated in some way.

Drought: You may be feeling emotionally drained.

Drum: Success may be in your future or you could be feeling that you are deserving more recognition.

E

Earthquake: You may be facing a difficulty in your life, or a major change may be about to occur.

Eating: You may be feeling a sense of strength and comfort.

Egg: You may be searching for creative inspiration.

Explosion: You may be fearful about something in your life that feels threatening.

F

Factory: You may want to "manufacture" a new image for yourself.

Falling: You may be fearful of failing at school.

Feather: Your troubles may be lightening.

Fence: You may be in need of more privacy in your life.

Fire: You may have some bottled-up anger about something or someone.

G

Garden: You may be feeling tremendous joy.

Giant: You may be focusing on a particular adult or authority figure in your life.

Gift: You may be about to experience good fortune in your life.

Gold: You may be focusing on an asset in your life such as your intelligence or athletic talent.

Grass: A general good sign of growth and prosperity.

H

Hair: You may be wishing for greater freedom in your life and fewer constraints.

Halo: You may be seeking spiritual guidance.

Hospital: You may need to slow down and take things easy.

Hotel: You may be thinking about a transition that is occurring in your life.

House: You may be focusing on yourself and wishing to create more stability in your world.

Hunger: You may be about to experience a major improvement in your life.

I

Ice: You may be worried about a friendship or relationship.

Invisibility: You may be feeling overlooked and undervalued.

Invitation: You may be hoping to make some more friends.

Island: You may be feeling lonely or hoping to escape. It could be you need to find more time for yourself.

J

Jackpot: You may be interested in finding a way to make some more money.

Jail: You may be feeling confined in some way or that your parents should be disciplining you.

Jewels: You may be thinking about things in your life that you feel have the most value.

Journey: You may be about to experience lots of personal growth and discovery.

Judge: You may be feeling guilty about something, or it may be a reminder that you need to be fair toward someone in your life.

Jungle: You may be feeling anxious about an upcoming event.

Jury: You may be concerned about the reaction you get from family and friends regarding something you have done recently.

K

Key: You may be in search of a solution to a problem that's been bothering you.

King: You may be looking for support or guidance from an adult in your life.

Kiss: You may be dwelling on feelings that you're hesitant to reveal to others.

Kite: You may be about to achieve a goal or be set free from a situation that's been holding you back in some way.

Knocking: You may need to ask someone you trust for some advice.

L

Ladder: You may be thinking about your wish to succeed and to "make it to the top."

Lake: If the lake in your dream is still, you may be feeling calm. If the water seems rough, you may be feeling troubled or you could be facing some emotional turbulence.

Letter: You may wish to communicate better with someone in your life.

Library: You may be struggling to process or understand some new information.

Litter: Your social life may be in a state of disarray.

M

Magic: You may need to be cautious of being misled by someone.

Maze: You may be trying to solve a complex problem.

Mirror: You may be concerned about your image and how you appear to others.

Mountain: You may be focusing on your goals and aspirations.

Music: You may be thinking about creativity. If the music sounds bad or out of tune, it could symbolize things in your life that aren't harmonious.

N

Naked: You may need to be more open about something that's troubling you.

Nests: You may be focusing a lot of attention on your family.

O

Ocean: You may feel that you're not experiencing enough fun in your life.

Old man or old woman: You may be seeking guidance or help from an elder. A calm and wise older person in a dream may be a sign that answers and insight are on their way.

Operation: You may wish to get rid of an unhappy situation in your life.

Orchestra: You might like to be in a leadership position.

P

Painting: You may feel that you have something to hide.

Palace: You may wish to feel more secure or be looking for more excitement in your life.

Path: You may feel that you aren't able to achieve what you want.

Police officer: You may be feeling insecure in some way and searching for some type of protection.

Q

Quarantine: You may be feeling isolated.

Quarrel: You may feel that a friendship has become boring and needs an added element of fun.

Queen: You may feel ignored and desire more attention.

Quicksand: You may feel that you are being drawn into a situation that you would rather steer away from.

R

Race: You may feel that you have a rival or competitor in your life.

Rainbow: You may feel things are full of promise or that good news is on its way.

Rescue: You may wish to change certain areas of your life.

Rope: You may be feeling restricted in some way.

Rose: You may be feeling love toward someone special in your life.

Running: You may wish to escape from a situation that's dragging you down.

S

School: You may not be feeling comfortable or not be giving your all to your studies.

Shell: You may be feeling shy or protective about someone.

Snow: You may be working through obstacles or going through some type of transformation.

Speech: You may have strong feelings about something that you've been unable to express to others.

Staircase: You may be on the way to accomplishing a major goal or achievement.

Storm: You may be anticipating a heated argument with someone you care about.

Swimming: You may be about to achieve a major success.

T

Teacher: You may be feeling that you can help others learn.

Television: You may feel that you've become too much of a spectator and need to become more involved and active in things.

Traffic: You may feel that you aren't making enough progress in some aspect of your life.

Trial: You may be feeling guilty about something or in search of an answer or "verdict" of some sort. Often in a trial dream, you are the judge and the jury.

U

Umbrella: You may feel that you need to protect or shield yourself from certain people in your life.

Uniform: You may be wishing that you fit in more with a certain circle of people.

University: Your subconscious may be reminding you that hard work will eventually pay off.

V

Vacation: You may wish to escape some of your everyday hassles, or perhaps you want a little more excitement in your life.

Veil: You may feel that there is something you need to hide.

Volcano: You may be feeling inner turmoil that you should pay attention to.

Voyage: You may feel that you should forge ahead with your plans.

W

Wall: You may feel that you are about to overcome an obstacle or get past something that's been holding you back.

Washing: You may be feeling guilty about something.

War: You may be feeling tension at home or with a friend.

X

X ray: You may be afraid of revealing your inner feelings to someone in your life.

Y

Yawn: You may be tired or bored with something that is happening in your life. It may signal that you should take action in some way.

Z

Zipper: You may wish to relax or make your life easier.

Zoo: You may be feeling confined or that you are under constant observation.

To Sleep,
Perchance
to Dream

Chapter Five
Sleep – Who Needs It?

Seems we all need sleep. Some people can get by on less sleep than others, but everyone needs plenty of rest. While some women (former British prime minister Margaret Thatcher and domestic diva Martha Stewart among them) claim they're able to get by on just four hours of sleep a night, most people need about eight hours of shut-eye to function well. When it comes to people, we sleep for about one-third of our lives!

And we're not alone — even fish need some sleep. (That's what they're doing when they hang out at the bottom of an aquarium!) Clams and crabs crash out on the ocean floor. And when a bird wants some downtime, it tucks its head under its wing. (Talk about a nice down comforter!) The larger creatures of the world need time to wind down, too. Elephants only spend about two and a half hours in a 24-hour time period sleeping, and they sleep standing up! Tigers, on the other hand, are into taking major catnaps. They log in a total of about sixteen hours of shut-eye a day!

Here's some news on naps:

Napping comes easiest after lunch because of post-meal drowsiness. Your body has two daily biological dips, one from 1 P.M. to 3 P.M.; the other from 2 A.M. to 4 A.M.

Naps are best when they last about twenty to thirty minutes.

Nap to increase endurance and performance. However, if you rely on naps too much, it may be a major signal that you're not getting enough sleep at night.

Thomas Edison could supposedly get by on two hours of sleep a night. But he was said to be very big on naps. Winston Churchill took a nap every afternoon, and so did American presidents Truman, Kennedy, and Johnson.

How Much Sleep Do You Need?

Your body has an internal clock that helps to create circadian rhythms. *Circa* means "about" and *dian* means "a day." Our twenty-four-hour daily routine takes on a rhythm of its own, which usually translates into sixteen hours of being awake and eight hours of being asleep. Studies have been done to determine if our awake/sleep patterns are just our way of reacting to the sun coming up in the morning and setting in the evening. But it turns out we all have internal clocks that "tell" us when we need to rest. How was this discovery made?

Researchers placed some volunteers in dark caves for weeks at a time (they agreed to participate!) and studied their sleep patterns. Even though these "cave dwellers" weren't experiencing any differences in light that would help them distinguish day from night, they still ended up falling into sleep patterns of about eight hours of sleep and sixteen hours of staying awake. Weird!

So, there's proof that our bodies definitely operate best when we get a certain amount of sleep. But why exactly do we need to sleep? Check out some of these blast-from-the-past theories:

- Ages ago, people believed that sleeping was when people put themselves in touch with the spirit world!
- The Greek philosopher Aristotle noticed that people seemed to fall asleep after eating big meals. So he figured we needed sleep to help us digest our food.
- Another popular sleep theory was that we sleep if our bodies are physically tired. But

if that theory held true, someone like Mia Hamm would need tons more sleep-time after a game than, say, a person who spent the day sitting at a desk. Totally not the case. So much for that theory!

So, what really is going on when we sleep? Turns out our bodies and brains just need a break — time to rest and recharge. When someone says, "I'm tired. I really need to recharge my batteries," that's exactly what being well rested is all about.

Welcome to the Sleep Lab

Before you begin to figure out your dreams, it helps to know some stuff about sleep. Okay, your head hits the pillow, and you're all set to hitch a ride to Snooze City. How exactly do you get to your desired destination? Here's the deal. In the course of a night, you go through four different stages of sleep, and then the whole sequence repeats itself — again and again.

Stage One is a light sleep in which your heartbeat slows, your muscles begin to relax, and your breathing becomes very even. At this stage of sleep, you can be easily awakened.

Stage Two is a deeper stage of light sleep.

Stage Three is known as "quiet sleep." Your heart slows even more and your blood pressure and body temperature drop. This is often called being in a sound sleep.

Stage Four is very deep sleep.

During a typical night of sleep, after your first set of dreams, you go through the stages of sleep again and begin another set of dreams. Since you go through the sleep cycle many times during a night, it's unlikely you can remember all the dreams you experience. Often you'll only remember the last dream you had. Your dreams usually occur about ninety minutes apart. And most people dream during about 20 percent of their sleep-time.

You Are Now Entering the Dream State

How can someone tell if you're dreaming? Your eyes move rapidly, or engage in REM, if you are in the dream stages of sleep. When you're in REM sleep, your heart rate is increased and your arms and legs are totally limp.

If you're deprived of your dream sleep, odds are you'll be in a major bad mood the next day. When people don't get enough non-REM sleep, they often feel sluggish and are often kind of clumsy the next day. But if they're deprived of REM sleep, they can be super-sensitive and often find it difficult to concentrate on new information and recall things. It's that dream sleep that helps you cope with stress and sort out all kinds of information in your brain.

Chapter Six
How to Get a Good Night's Sleep

So you skip some sleep. Is it really all that bad to bail on sticking to a reasonable bedtime? Is feeling groggy as you head off to school such a horrible thing? Well, experts at the Sleep Disorder Center for Children in Dallas say millions of kids aren't doing well in school because they're sleep-deprived. It's believed that kids today are getting an hour less sleep per night than kids did in years past.

Without enough sleep, your mood, memory, and ability to concentrate suffer and your stress level soars. It was found that the grade point averages of eighth- and ninth-graders who had trouble sleeping was lower than those who got a good night's sleep. And tired high school students are at a higher risk for mood and behavior problems and even drug abuse. Scary stuff! On the flip side, high-achieving high school students sleep at least eight hours a night, much more than the weeknight average of six to seven hours. How much is enough?

Check out this chart to see how age can make a difference in how much sleep you need:

Nursery schoolers	Age 3 to 4	11 to 12 hours
Elementary schoolers	Age 5 to 10	10 to 11 hours
Middle schoolers	Age 11 to 14	9 1/4 to 10 hours
High schoolers	Age 15 to 18	8 1/2 to 9 hours

Keep in mind that some seriously important stuff is going on when you're down for the count. And sleep experts are becoming more and more convinced that an eighth hour of sleep provides a big-time bonus for your brain and your body. Being well rested is like a secret strategy to fight off stress and irritability.

Fight Fatigue!

Ever have one of those days when you feel totally wiped out? The amount of energy you feel you have to face the day is usually a combination of the energy you wake up with in the morning (think of this as your reserve fuel tank) combined with the things in your life that give you energy and the things going on in your life that seem to steal it away. Some stuff that can zap you of energy include being sick, feeling stressed about school or certain relationships, and bad habits such as eating a lot of junk food. Energy boosters include good eating habits, getting restful sleep each night, and feeling good about the things that are going on in your life.

And here's another thing. If you want to keep going and going like the Energizer Bunny, you should get some exercise during the day. Experts feel that aerobic exercise is one of the best ways to fight off fatigue. The other cool deal about exercise is that it improves the way you feel about yourself. While you might think it's all in your head, it's also a real-deal occurrence! Your body releases endorphins that can make you feel happier and more relaxed. If you're in good spirits, you have a much better chance at fighting fatigue.

Here are some better-sleep basics:

First and foremost, establish a regular bedtime routine. When you were little, odds are an adult in your life encouraged you to get into your pajamas, brush your teeth, and choose a bedtime story. Then after being read to, you would start to snooze. That sense of routine helps people of all ages.

Lots of people watch tons of TV before going to bed, but experts say one of the best pre-bedtime activities to choose is taking a warm bath or shower.

Pamper yourself with a beauty treatment such as putting lotion on your feet or hands.

Keep a journal to help you slow down. One of the ways you can turn even the most stressful day into a restful one is to make a list of five to ten best things that happened during your day.

Here are some other before-bedtime tips:

DON'T eat a heavy meal right before bed.

DO have a light carbohydrate snack such as toast or some crackers and jam about 45 minutes before bedtime. This type of snack will help produce serotonin, a brain chemical that triggers sleep. You know how you feel completely sleepy after feasting on Thanksgiving? Certain foods that are full of protein, such as turkey, milk, cheese, and sweets like honey, jam, or jelly cause a chemical called tryptophan to kick into gear. It's like a natural sleep-inducer. Avoid snacks that are heavy or rich. Those foods can take longer to digest, and that can delay or disrupt your sleep.

Some people feel that eating super-spicy foods can cause you to have bad dreams. Not really true. But it is true that super-spicy food or food that's hard for your body to digest can make it more difficult for you to fall asleep. And if you're spending too much time tossing and turning trying to get to sleep, you won't get a good night's sleep. When you wake up in the morning feeling not exactly well rested, it's pretty easy to point the blame at the food you ate the night before.

DON'T drink beverages with caffeine. That includes coffee, tea, colas, and chocolate.

DO drink a cup of herbal tea such as chamomile tea.

DO take a warm bath. Soaking in warm water before bed causes your body temperature to drop, which helps you doze off.

DON'T exercise intensely before bedtime. Exercise is great for you. And if you work out on a regular basis, you'll sleep better because it helps you reduce stress and anxiety. But the best time for working out is several hours before bedtime. When you exercise, you raise your body's temperature. Sleep researchers know that right before you're about to fall asleep, your body temperature tends to drop about half a degree. This small shift in temperature triggers a whole chain of events that bring on sleep.

It's best to work out in the late afternoon or early evening, which gives your body a chance to cool down by bedtime. That way when your temperature drops, you'll be all set to sleep.

DO some stretches. To help yourself enter a stress-free slumber zone after a long day that's left you feeling kind of wired, try some deep breathing and simple yoga moves to loosen your muscles. You'll increase your flexibility and feel much calmer.

Here's a before-bed stretching routine that can help improve your flexibility: Stand with your legs as wide apart as possible, keeping your back straight. Balance your body weight on your heels and put your hands on your hips, then slide your hands down to the tops of your thighs. While you're doing this, exhale through your nose. Keep moving your hands down your legs until they reach your calves, elongating your back as you go. Hold for about fifteen seconds, breathing shallowly, and increasing the stretch if you're able to. Inhale slowly and deeply, rounding your spine and gradually returning your arms and torso to your starting position.

Here's another simple stretch: Lie facedown, flat on the floor, with your elbows bent and your palms at shoulder level. Inhale as you lift your forehead off the floor, then your chin, shoulders, and chest. Using your arms and back, support your torso. Hold for fifteen seconds and focus on creating a long, rounded curve with your spine. Exhale as you bend your arms and slowly lower your body back to the floor.

DON'T read scary stories or get into heated arguments with anyone.

DO read some poetry or inspirational reading.

DON'T listen to loud music.

DO create a quiet, restful environment. A whole bunch of background noise can make it hard for you to get to sleep. If there's still a lot going on in your household after your bedtime, consider filtering out the background noise with some "white noise" or sounds, which will both muffle the noise and provide soothing sounds. A fan or air conditioner can do the trick. You may also want to try a tape of soothing sounds from nature such as those made by ocean waves or heard in a tropical rain forest.

DON'T force yourself to stay in bed if you can't get to sleep. Give yourself about fifteen minutes to nod off. Want some mental exercises that can help if you're having trouble falling asleep? Recite a poem. Think of the first and last names of all the students in your class. You can also concentrate on relaxing your entire body starting at your toes and working your way up to your neck and head. Aim for a completely relaxed state.

DO sleep on a comfortable mattress. Remember that fairy tale about the princess and the pea? She slept on a towering stack of mattresses and was so sensitive to her surroundings (or was such a light sleeper) that she could detect a pea that had been placed beneath the bottom mattress. Like that sleeping beauty — and that girl named Goldilocks — you'll want to have a bed that's not too hard, not too soft . . . one that's just right!

Ideally, your bed should have a solid, thick mattress that can do a good job of supporting your back. If your mattress is way too soft, it can be hard for you to get into a position that feels comfortable.

When it comes to pillow talk, there are all kinds of 'em out there. There are super-soft pillows stuffed with goose and duck feathers and firmer ones that are made of foam or other synthetic materials. Some people are incredibly allergic to feather pillows, and if you're one of them, you'll want to avoid down pillows so you can spend your time snoozing instead of sneezing! As for how many pillows work best, that, too, is a matter of personal preference. If you find yourself rearranging pillows and moving piles of your favorite stuffed animals around a lot, you may need to clear some more sleep space for yourself.

DO turn off your computer and put your backpack and that big stack of schoolbooks out of sight. You don't want to go to bed thinking about all that's on your plate for tomorrow.

DO consider scenting your bedroom with scents that have been linked with helping people sleep. Two to try are apple and vanilla. Consider placing some scented potpourri or an unlit candle on your nightstand, or rub some scented vanilla lotion on your hands before you go to sleep.

DON'T have a morning alarm clock that's super-loud or startling. A clock radio that switches on mellow music or a soothing voice makes more morning sense.

DO wake to light. As soon as you wake up, let the sunshine in. Get a dose of morning light by opening up your curtains or blinds.

Get Your Beauty Sleep

Nighttime is the prime time for getting gorgeous. While you sleep, your body rests and your skin has an opportunity to regenerate and renew itself. It's your body's chance to recharge.

Save Face

You definitely want to wash your face before you put it on your pillowcase. You're gonna be snoozing for several hours and you don't want dirt to do a number on your skin all through the night. Wash away the day's dirt and grime and clean your complexion.

Spot Treatment

If you're being bugged by breakouts, night-time is the right time to fight back in a big way. Apply some acne medication to the trouble spots and let the ingredients combat your complexion flare-ups while you sleep.

Nail Call

Dry cuticles can be a real drag. Work some cuticle oil or hand lotion into your cuticles and on your hands and let those moisturizing ingredients sink in as you sleep. Also, be sure to drink lots of water every day (at least eight glasses).

Foot Patrol

Lots of celebs have been known to use this trick to get super-smooth feet. Slather your feet with foot lotion or petroleum jelly and then slip into a pair of clean cotton socks. When you wake up, your feet will feel soft and smooth. They'll

have had the whole night to soak up a rich re-
ward.

Conclusion

Now that you're more in tune with the night voyages you take whenever you go to sleep, put your dreams to work for you! Use your dreams as tools to tap into your creativity, as opportunities for you to figure out how to get along better with your family and friends, and, most important, to learn more about yourself.

Follow your dreams. . . . There are no limits to where they can take you. And now that you're equipped with all kinds of nocturnal knowledge, there's no reason you can't make the most of all your dreams. Here's wishing you sweet dreams and hoping that all your dreams come true!